ALPHABET KNOWLEDGE

CONTENTS

About this book

Alphabet Knowledge contains a collection of practical ideas for learning letter sounds and names built around the use of an A1 poster of an 'Alphabet train'. The book is divided into four sections which show a progression of activities suitable for a range of abilities in Key Stage 1/P1–3. The activities are quick, fun ideas that will encourage confidence and mastery of letter sounds, letter names, letter formation and alphabetical order. In many ways this occasional 'opportunistic' reinforcement can be likened to practising mental recall skills for mathematics.

About the poster

The full-colour side of the poster shows a train, each truck containing an animal which has a particular beginning letter sound, with upper and lower case letters clearly displayed on the sides of the trucks. The coloured truck wheels encourage the children to differentiate between vowels and consonants. Segmented wheels highlight the consonant 'y', which often masquerades as a vowel. The poster includes pictures of a cheetah, a sheep and a thrush in a tree which will help children to identify the sounds 'ch', 'sh', 'th' and 'tr'.

The black and white side of the poster provides a map of the farm from the story *The Snow Lambs* by Debi Gliori (André Deutsch Children's Books), and encourages the children to use upper and lower case letters to identify significant features. The alphabet jigsaw puzzle should enable children to become confident with the letter order – the order in which the letters of the alphabet are spoken and written – and it should help to reinforce letter sounds.

The Literacy Hour

These activities are ideally suited for the word-level strand of the Literacy Hour or for a final reinforcement at the end of the plenary. Alphabet work is mentioned in the National Literacy Strategy *Framework for Teaching* throughout Key Stage 1. Most of the work in this book is aimed at Years R and 1 (P1 and 2) because the NLS identifies this as being essential learning for the youngest children in school. Using dictionaries, indexes, glossaries and other alphabetically ordered texts appears in Year 2 (P3).

INTRODUCTION

Word-level work:

Reception year
2 Knowledge of grapheme/phoneme correspondences through: ◆ hearing and identifying initial sounds in words ◆ reading letter(s) that represent(s) the sound(s): *a-z, ch, sh, th* ◆ writing each letter in response to each sound: *a-z, ch, sh, th* ◆ identifying and writing initial and dominant phonemes in spoken words ◆ identifying and writing initial and final phonemes in consonant-vowel-consonant (CVC) words.
3 Alphabetic and phonic knowledge through: ◆ sounding and naming each letter of the alphabet in lower and upper case ◆ writing letters in response to letter names ◆ understanding alphabetic order through alphabet books, rhymes and songs.
4 To link sound and spelling patterns by: ◆ identifying alliteration in known and new and invented words.

Year 1 Term 1
2 From YR, to practise and secure alphabetic letter knowledge and alphabetic order.
4 To discriminate and segment all three phonemes in CVC words.

The use of these skills is developed in Year 2 through text-level work:

Year 2 Term 2
16 To use dictionaries and glossaries to locate words by using initial letter.
18 To use other alphabetically ordered texts, eg indexes, directories, listings, registers; to discuss how they are used.
20 To make class dictionaries and glossaries of special interest words…

Year 2 Term 3
15 To use a contents page and index to find way about text.

About teaching letter names and sounds

Before children are exposed to the written code (sound picture*), it is essential that they are able to identify the beginning sound in words. English is a difficult language, so initially you should choose words that have a definite sound at the beginning of the word. If possible, choose words with one consonant rather than a blend (the word 'top' rather than 'tree', for example).

Children enjoy making sounds. Ask the children to look at one another making the sounds or use plastic mirrors, if these are available. Ask the children: 'What shape is your mouth making when you say "mmm"; what about "b, b, b"? Which one makes a long sound; which one makes a very short sound?' Try to prevent the children adding the 'uh' sound after the sounds, especially in the explosive sounds, for example, /c/ not 'cuh.' This type of activity will encourage the children to concentrate on the sounds that can be heard at the beginning of words.

Play 'Odd sound out': say about four words, one of which should have a different beginning letter to the other three. Ask the children which beginning sound is different. Once they have become confident at hearing and matching these beginning sounds (some that are difficult to differentiate like 'd' and 't' may take longer), the written code can be introduced.

Learning letter shapes to represent our spoken sounds

Letters do not make sounds; we make sounds and the letters are a code for recording that sound. Matching sounds with the letter (sound picture*) can be difficult. However, it is easier once you can identify the sound you are making. Most classrooms have a pictorial alphabet. The A1 poster in this book will help, as the children will be able to match the beginning sound they are voicing to the animal and then the truck letter. Children need to practise writing the letter at the same time. You may find it easier with big hand movements in the air and using appropriate directions, for example:

◆ *For 'h', start at the top, go down, then halfway back up, curve over and down.*

◆ *When we say 'mmm', we write this letter…*

Handwriting practice photocopiable sheets, to help the children to write the letters, are provided on pages 27–29. If you wish to give the children more experience of a particular letter shape, sections of these sheets can be photocopied, cut and pasted into new photocopiable masters.

INTRODUCTION

What is an alphabet?

An alphabet is a code that represents letter names. Some of these represent the sounds that we make as we speak, others are merely the names given to the sounds in speech. These letters have been arranged as an alphabet; the order helps us to memorize the single letter names.

In English, we have 44 phonemes but only 26 letters to represent the sounds in words. Combining letters in clusters or using the same letter to make different sounds creates the additional sounds.

When speaking we don't need to know that 'th' in 'think' and 'th' in 'this' are written with the same letter combination – similarly, that 'c' as in 'cake' can be written as 'ck' in 'sick' and 'k' in 'kite'. However, the written (grapheme) representation makes reading and writing more difficult. We need to know the sound to make and in some cases the variations. The 'ea' in 'head' is not the same sound as the 'ea' in 'ear'; and letter combinations may look different, as in 'ow' in 'owl' and 'ou' in 'loud', but make the same sound.

Much of this is historical, our language having evolved over time, enriched and influenced by other languages. The disadvantage is that it can be difficult to master, and decoding – understanding the visual code of the letters – is problematic.

Learning the alphabet names is important in our culture, and children are praised for knowing the correct letter order. If we don't know the order it is impossible to use a dictionary, locate an entry in an alphabetically arranged encyclopaedia, use an index or find a number in the telephone directory.

Ideas for display

Children enjoy making their own alphabets. Compile an alphabet book – of animals, things to eat, items to be found in the home and so on. They love painting themselves; use their names and an alliterative picture, for example: Alice acting angrily, Jonathan jumping jerkily, Mary munching mussels. You will need to invent some for 'missing' letters, so the children could use characters from stories or television.

Further and useful reading references

Resource Bank English KS1/P1–3: Spelling and Phonics Charlotte Reeve (Scholastic) – fun but practical approaches to teaching phonemes including an A1 poster illustrating the sounds

Primary Professional Bookshelf: How to teach reading Nicholas Bielby (Scholastic)

* *Why children can't read: and what we can do about it* Diane McGuinness (Penguin) – uses the term 'sound pictures' for letters.

LET'S LOOK AT THE POSTER

GROUP SIZE AND ORGANIZATION
Whole class sitting in a semicircle.
DURATION
10–20 minutes.
LEARNING OBJECTIVE
To learn the letter names and alphabet order.

YOU WILL NEED
The 'Alphabet train' poster.

WHAT TO DO
You may like to introduce the poster folded up and build up the excitement by guessing what it might show. Unfold it slowly as the children guess. They may be familiar with alphabet nursery friezes – some may have one in their bedroom. Ask the children questions such as:

◆ *What does the poster show?* (Animals, a train, an alphabet…)
◆ *Which animals can you see/name?* (Alligator… and so on. Don't worry about order at this stage.)
◆ *How many are there? Let's count them up.* (26.)
◆ *Are they all different?* (Yes!)
◆ *What's written on each truck?*
◆ *How do the letters match the animals?* (One for every letter.) *Hmm… I think this is an alphabet train. The words we read and write are made up from letters. Each of the letters we use to make words has a different shape and a special sound or sounds: /p/, /f/, /d/; and has a name: p, f, d.*

You may like to go on to point to each letter and give it a name and talk about the sound(s) it represents – concentrating initially on, for example, 'The "a" in alligator sounds like /a/.'

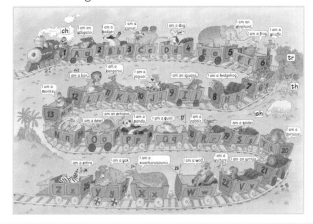

LETTER NAMES

ALPHABET LETTER NAME ORDER

GROUP SIZE AND ORGANIZATION
Whole class sitting in a semicircle facing the poster (YR/Y1; P1/2).
DURATION
Five minutes.
LEARNING OBJECTIVE
To learn the letter names and alphabet order.

YOU WILL NEED
The 'Alphabet train' poster, a ruler or similar safe 'pointer'.

WHAT TO DO
Choose a child to use the ruler to point to each truck on the poster as the children recite the alphabet in unison: 'a, b, c…' and so on. Then ask the children to take turns to say the letter names, saying them one after each other, in the order in which they are sitting in the semicircle.

Vary the task by beginning at different places along the alphabet.

ASSESSMENT
Watch to make sure all the children are able to join in with the chant, as the whole group recites the alphabet.

JIGSAW LETTERS

GROUP SIZE AND ORGANIZATION
All the children sitting in a semicircle at the beginning and the end of the activity; working in pairs at tables for the craft-based part of the activity (YR/Y1; P1/2).
DURATION
Five minutes for the introduction, then 20 minutes for working in pairs. You may want to discuss the finished jigsaws for a further five minutes.
LEARNING OBJECTIVES
To recognize the letters of the alphabet. To be able to arrange the letters in sequence.

YOU WILL NEED
'Jigsaw snake' black and white poster, photocopies of the 'snake' poster (one for each pair of children), scissors, glue, large sheets of art paper for sticking down the children's completed snakes..

WHAT TO DO
Ask the children questions such as:
◆ *What can you see on this poster?*
◆ *How many segments does the snake have? Who can come out to check?*
◆ *Shall we read the segments together?*
◆ *What do you notice?*
◆ *What will we need to do to put the snake in alphabetical order?*
◆ *Which letter will you need first/second… last on our snake?*
◆ *Do you think the snake is going to go in a long line or in a twisted shape?*
◆ *Is it wise to begin sticking before putting all the letters in the right order?*
◆ *What will you need to do before sticking your snake? How will you check?*

Hand out the photocopies of the snake poster for the children to cut out and arrange in order. When the children are ready to stick down the sections, remind them to ask an adult to help them check the order. When each pair has made a snake picture, regroup and read the alliterative snake sections together.

ASSESSMENT
Are the children able to recognize the letters and arrange them in alphabetical order?

EXTENSION WORK
You could use this activity to extend 'What do our names begin with?' on page 16: 'I am amazing Alison', 'I am bouncy Bobby' and so on. Further ideas can be added as the children become more confident: 'I am sensible Sam sitting on a soft sofa.' These sentences could be typed out on the computer, illustrated with clip art and used as a classroom alphabet. (See the display ideas on page 3.)

ORDER THE CARDS

GROUP SIZE AND ORGANIZATION
Whole class sitting in a semicircle facing the poster (YR/Y1; P1/2).
DURATION
Five to ten minutes.
LEARNING OBJECTIVES
To be able to arrange letters in alphabetical order. To begin to be aware of the location of a particular letter in the order.

YOU WILL NEED
An alphabet card for each child, photocopied from pages 8–12 (if you have more than 26 children you will need doubles of some letters; this game can be played with lower case, upper case or a combination of upper and lower case letters), the 'Alphabet train' poster (optional).

WHAT TO DO
Deal out the letter cards, one per child. Ask the children to see how quickly they can arrange themselves in alphabetical/the right order. (This would also be suitable for a PE warm-up activity.)
◆ *Which letter comes first?*
◆ *Think, before you start moving – is your letter one that comes at the beginning, near the middle or near the end of the alphabet?*
◆ *Put your hand up if your letter comes before 'g'. Will you be near the beginning or at the end of the line?*
  Once the children are in order, ask them:
◆ *Can you each say your letter name and sound as we go round the circle?*
  You could use the 'Alphabet train' poster for checking the order. Collect in the cards, shuffle and re-deal them, maybe concentrating on end or middle position letters.

ASSESSMENT
Do all the children have some idea as to where in the alphabet their letters might come: near the beginning, in the middle or at the end?

Using the 'Snow Lambs' map
You may want to read and discuss the storybook *The Snow Lambs* by Debi Gliori (André Deutsch Children's Books) before trying the following three activities. The original coloured map is used on the endpapers of the hardback edition. (A big book version of the story and supporting literacy texts are also published by Scholastic.) Animals to photocopy and position on the map with Blu-Tack are also supplied on the poster, though you may prefer to draw your own (or print them with stamps) onto Post-it notes.

HOW CAN I FIND PLACES ON THE MAP?

GROUP SIZE AND ORGANIZATION
A group of about ten children (Y1/2; P2/3).
DURATION
15 minutes.
LEARNING OBJECTIVES
To improve familiarity with alphabetical order, both upper and lower case letters. To be able to find positions on a map using letter co-ordinates.

YOU WILL NEED
The 'Snow Lambs map' poster, a flip chart or a sheet of paper pinned up nearby, marker pen.

WHAT TO DO
Ask the children:
◆ *What do we call this type of picture?* (A map.)
◆ *Why do you think we call this picture a map?*
◆ *What can you see on the map?*
◆ *How do we find places on a map?*
◆ *Why do you think this map has lines going across and down?* (You may want to call them horizontal and vertical lines.)
◆ *Why do you think there are letters along the horizontal and vertical lines at the edges/axes?*
◆ *Who can find Star Woods on the map?*
◆ *Which squares is it in? If I write 'Star Woods is in squares...', what do you think I might write?*
  Explain that you always read co-ordinates by going across and then up ('along the hallway and then up the stairs').
  Find other places on the map. Write their co-ordinates. Conclude the lesson by finding places using the co-ordinates: 'What is in square (L, t)?'

LETTER NAMES

ASSESSMENT
Are the children able to read and use the alphabetical letters comfortably? (Check that they are always using the horizontal letter before reading the vertical letter.)

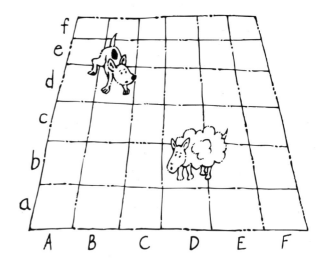

PUT THE ANIMAL IN THE SQUARE

GROUP SIZE AND ORGANIZATION
A group of about ten children (Y1/2; P2/3).
DURATION
15 minutes.
LEARNING OBJECTIVE
To increase familiarity with using the alphabet by placing animal pictures in the map squares and reading letter co-ordinates.

YOU WILL NEED
The 'Snow Lambs map' poster, a flip chart or a sheet of paper pinned up nearby with prepared statements (for example: Put the dog in [B, b]), small Post-it notes with farm animals drawn on them (or printed using animal stamps) or animal cards photocopied from the poster (and Blu-Tack).

WHAT TO DO
Read the first statement from the chart and ask:
◆ *Who can point to the square where the dog needs to go?*
◆ *Is that the right square?*
◆ *How do we know?*
  Choose a child to position the dog. Then repeat with the other animals and statements.
  Conclude the activity by turning over the chart of statements and asking the children to tell you where the animals are positioned:
◆ *Who can tell me where the sheep is positioned?*
◆ *Who can write the co-ordinate?* (Check by looking at the chart.)

ASSESSMENT
Can the children locate and identify squares on a map by using co-ordinates and write them correctly?
  It is important that the children rehearse 'along the hall and up the stairs' as this is a useful reminder of how to use co-ordinates. Remember, however, that this is an alphabet task, so focus on the letter recognition and writing skills, rather than the pre-maths or geography involved.

WHERE ARE THE ANIMALS?

GROUP SIZE AND ORGANIZATION
A group of about ten children (Y1/2; P2/3).
DURATION
15 minutes.
LEARNING OBJECTIVE
To practise writing letters (as co-ordinates on a map).

YOU WILL NEED
The 'Snow Lambs map' poster, a flip chart or a sheet of paper pinned up nearby, small Post-it notes with farm animals drawn on them (or printed using animal stamps) or animal cards photocopied from the poster (and Blu-Tack) – positioned on the map in advance, marker pen, paper, pencils.

WHAT TO DO
Ask the children to write down the co-ordinates for the animals and then to write a co-ordinate for repositioning one of the animals. Check by asking individual children to come out to write the co-ordinates required on the chart. Conclude by asking individual children to set a task verbally for another child. For example: Stacey asks, 'Can William put the cat in (W, p)?'

ASSESSMENT
Focus on the children's ability to write the co-ordinates correctly. Concentrate on the writing rather than the geography needed.

LETTER NAMES

CODES

GROUP SIZE AND ORGANIZATION
Whole class facing the 'Alphabet train' poster, then at tables in pairs or working alone (Y2; P3).
DURATION
Ten minutes explanation, then 20 minutes for the children to solve their own codes.
LEARNING OBJECTIVE
To become familiar with alphabetical order and have some 'feel' for the ordinal position of each letter.

YOU WILL NEED
A flip chart or a large sheet of paper, marker pen, the 'Alphabet train' poster, a copy of photocopiable page 13 for each child or pair, pencils.

WHAT TO DO
Before the lesson begins, write a short coded sentence on the flip chart. For example:

There is a donkey in truck number four.
20, 8, 5, 18, 5 / 9, 19 / 1 / 4, 15, 14, 11, 5, 25 / 9, 14 / 20, 18, 21, 3, 11 / 14, 21, 13, 2, 5, 18 / 6, 15, 21, 18.

Look at the code together and ask the children:
◆ *What do you think the numbers could represent?* (*The poster might give you a clue.*) (The ordinal position of the trucks on the 'Alphabet train' poster.)
◆ *Can you see a number that matches a truck?* (20 is a 't' – write the letter under the number.)
◆ *Can you see the number 20 anywhere else?* (Fill in the other 't'.)
◆ *What do you think we will need to do next?*
Encourage the children to crack the code systematically. There are several strategies that could be encouraged. For example, go through the alphabet, writing in 'a' for 1, 'b' for 2…; use the '20' to help crack the codes of letters more than 20 and so on.

The children should now work in pairs on a photocopied code sheet.

At the end of the activity you may want to select pairs to write their own codes on the flip chart for the class to solve.

ASSESSMENT
Answers for photocopiable page 13: 1. cat, 2. house, 3. bucket, 4. school, 5. teacher, 6. book, 7. mummy. Are the children sufficiently familiar with the alphabet to be able to locate a letter quickly on the alphabet?

LETTER NAMES

Upper and lower case letter cards

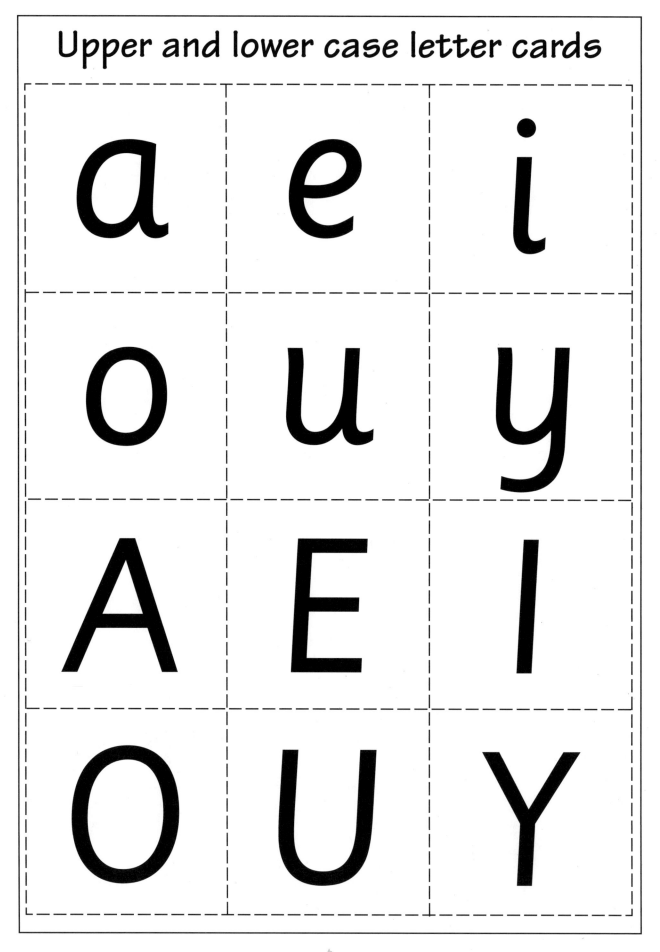

a	e	i
o	u	y
A	E	I
O	U	Y

ALPHABET KNOWLEDGE

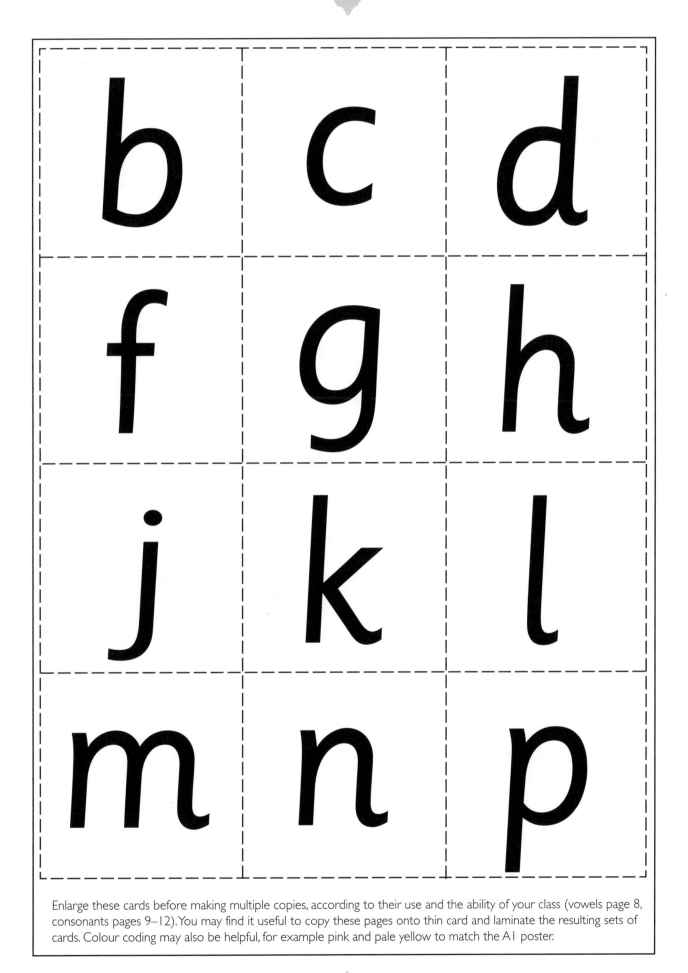

Enlarge these cards before making multiple copies, according to their use and the ability of your class (vowels page 8, consonants pages 9–12). You may find it useful to copy these pages onto thin card and laminate the resulting sets of cards. Colour coding may also be helpful, for example pink and pale yellow to match the A1 poster.

PHOTOCOPIABLE
RESOURCE
BANK

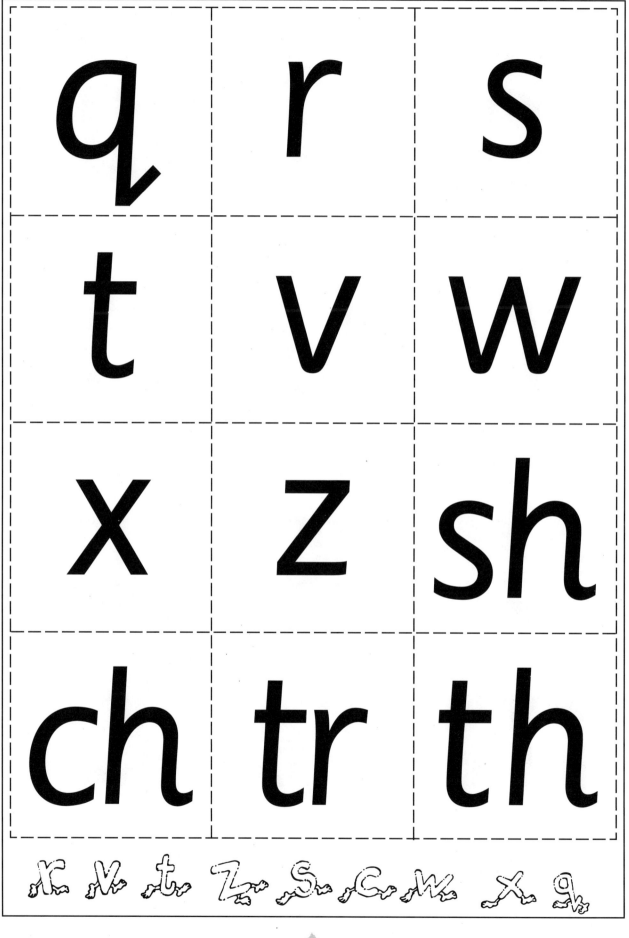

q r s
t v w
x z sh
ch tr th

PHOTOCOPIABLE
RESOURCE
BANK

ALPHABET KNOWLEDGE

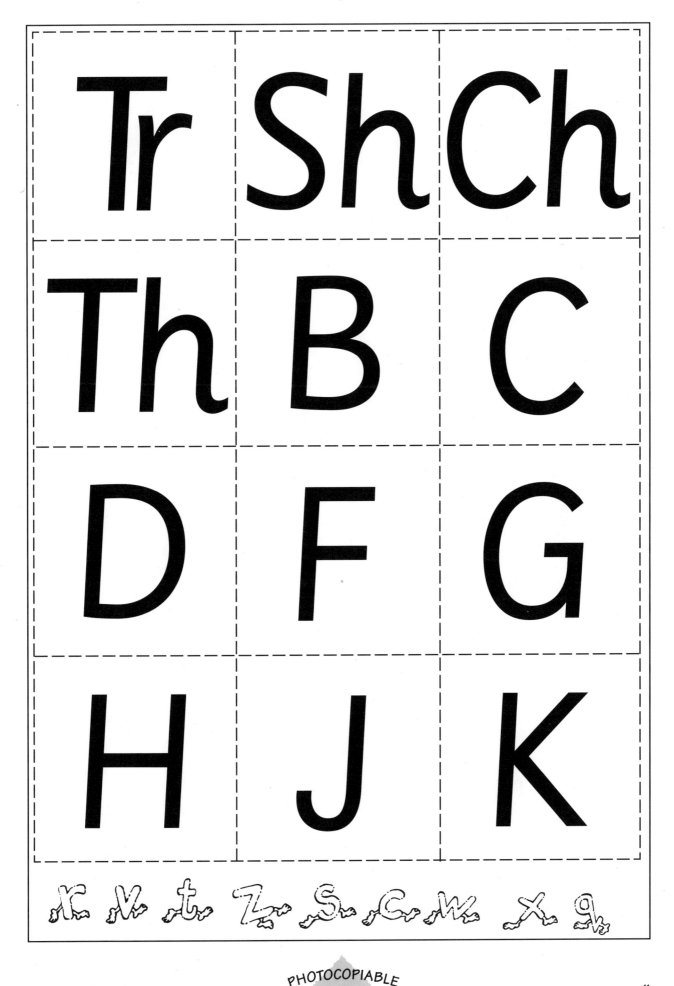

Tr	Sh	Ch
Th	B	C
D	F	G
H	J	K

K N t Z S C W X g

LETTER NAMES

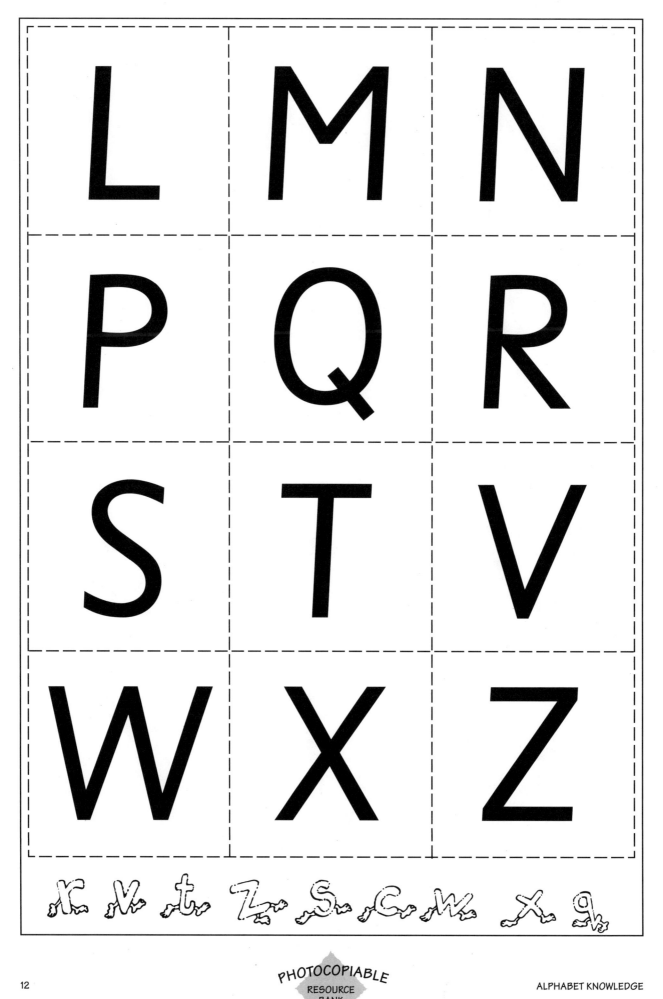

ALPHABET KNOWLEDGE

Name _____ Date _____

Codes

1. | 3 | 1 | 20 |
| --- | --- | --- |
| | | |

2. | 8 | 15 | 21 | 19 | 5 |
| --- | --- | --- | --- | --- |
| | | | | |

3. | 2 | 21 | 3 | 11 | 5 | 20 |
| --- | --- | --- | --- | --- | --- |
| | | | | | |

4. | 19 | 3 | 8 | 15 | 15 | 12 |
| --- | --- | --- | --- | --- | --- |
| | | | | | |

5. | 20 | 5 | 1 | 3 | 8 | 5 | 18 |
| --- | --- | --- | --- | --- | --- | --- |
| | | | | | | |

6. | 2 | 15 | 15 | 11 |
| --- | --- | --- | --- |
| | | | |

7. | 13 | 21 | 13 | 13 | 25 |
| --- | --- | --- | --- | --- |
| | | | | |

◆ Write the code for your name.

◆ Write the code for your birthday month.

◆ Find a word in your book and write the code for this word.

◆ Ask a friend to 'break your codes'.

LETTER SOUNDS

Ordering the sounds

ALPHABET LETTER SOUND ORDER

W

GROUP SIZE AND ORGANIZATION
Whole class sitting in a semicircle facing the poster (YR/Y1; P1/2).
DURATION
Ten minutes.
LEARNING OBJECTIVE
To learn that the sounds we make can be written as letters.

YOU WILL NEED
The 'Alphabet train' poster, a ruler or similar safe 'pointer'.

WHAT TO DO
Ask a child to come out to point to each letter as the children say: 'a is for alligator, b is for badger, c is for camel…' and so on. Then ask the children to say the letter sounds that begin each animal's name, speaking in turns in the order in which they are sitting in the semicircle. Emphasize that there is no need to say the whole name of the animal, just the first letter sound.

ASSESSMENT
Check that all the children can make the correct sound for each letter.

PICTURE ORDER

W

GROUP SIZE AND ORGANIZATION
Whole class sitting in a semicircle facing the poster (YR/Y1; P1/2).
DURATION
Ten minutes.
LEARNING OBJECTIVE
To enable the children to be able to establish alphabetical order by listening to the first sound in a spoken word.

YOU WILL NEED
The 'Alphabet train' poster, picture cards representing the letter sounds and names, photocopied from pages 21–23 (there are 36 cards; you may only want to use pictures of words that use the initial letter sound – 'a' for 'apple…' – and incorporate those sounding the letter names – 'a' for 'apron…' – later).

WHAT TO DO
Deal out the cards, one for each child. Ask the children to look at their cards carefully and try to order themselves like the alphabet, thinking about where their letter sounds fit in the alphabet. Can they arrange themselves in the right order?

Use the 'Alphabet train' poster for checking; each child should be encouraged to say something like, 'This is a cage starting with a "c" (or a circle starting with a "c").'

Then shuffle the cards and let everyone try again.

ASSESSMENT
Identify those children who find the task difficult and make sure they are given letters that are easier to position (for example, continuing to use the most common sounds) until they have gained in confidence.

RESOURCE BANK

LETTER SOUNDS

ALPHABET PAIRS

GROUP SIZE AND ORGANIZATION
A group of about four children sitting in a circle (YR/Y1; P1/2).
DURATION
About ten minutes.
LEARNING OBJECTIVE
To match initial letter sounds with corresponding pictures (other objectives are possible depending on the pairing involved – see 'What to do').

YOU WILL NEED
About ten letter cards and their matching pictures (chosen and photocopied from pages 8–12 and 21–23).

WHAT TO DO
Shuffle the letter and picture cards together and place them face down in rows. Let the children take turns to pick up two cards. If the letter sound and the picture match, the pair may be kept. If not, the cards must be put back in the position from where they were taken.

Variations on this game can be played to:
◆ revise the first ten letters learned
◆ refresh the children's memory of random letters
◆ pair up lower case with upper case letters.

ASSESSMENT
How quickly can the children match the pairs? Which letters need extra rehearsal?

WHICH LETTERS ARE HIDING?

GROUP SIZE AND ORGANIZATION
Whole class sitting in a semicircle facing the poster (YR/Y1; P1/2).
DURATION
Ten minutes.
LEARNING OBJECTIVES
To be able to identify hidden letters by knowing the alphabet order. To be able to write those letters.

YOU WILL NEED
The 'Alphabet train' poster (with Post-it notes placed over some trucks), a flip chart or a large sheet of paper, marker pen.

WHAT TO DO
Ask the children questions such as:
◆ *What sound does the first letter that has been covered up make?* ('b'.)
◆ *How do you know?* ('b' comes after 'a'.)
◆ *Which creature is sitting in the truck?* (Badger.)
◆ *Can you think of another word beginning with this letter?* (Banana, box, balloon, for example.)
◆ *What is the name of the letter?*
◆ *Who thinks they can come out to write the hidden letter on the paper?* (When a child has written the letter, remove the Post-it note for everyone to check.) *Let's all write the letter shape in the air. Top to bottom, halfway back up and round. It says 'b'. Can you feel your lips going together as you make the /b/ sound?*

Repeat this process with other letters. You could concentrate on similar letter shapes such as the 'c' writing family.

ASSESSMENT
Check that all the children can make the correct sounds and write the letter for the hidden letters. You may want to see how efficiently they are using their knowledge of the alphabet to identify the letters.

IDEAS FOR DIFFERENTIATION
You may need to check the sounds articulated. It sometimes helps to mispronounce the letter yourself – the children will quickly spot your mistake! Checking on the children's mouth shapes and the position of their tongues when speaking will help.

LETTER SOUNDS

Beginning sounds

WHAT DO OUR NAMES BEGIN WITH?

GROUP SIZE AND ORGANIZATION
Whole class sitting in a semicircle facing the poster (YR/Y1; P1/2).
DURATION
Ten minutes.
LEARNING OBJECTIVES
To recognize the upper case forms of the letters. To be able to arrange their names in alphabetical order, looking especially at upper case letters.

YOU WILL NEED
The 'Alphabet train' poster, Post-it notes.

WHAT TO DO
Go around the semicircle, asking each child to say their name and what their name begins with, for example: 'I am Sam. My name begins with "S".'

Then ask the children questions such as:
◆ *Does anyone have a name beginning with the first letter of the alphabet?* (Ask this child to move to sit at one end of the semicircle).
◆ *Who do you think should come next? Let's try to find the right order for you all to sit in to be in alphabetical order.* (Work systematically through the letters to re-seat each child. If there are no children whose names begin with 'A', move on to 'B'; if there is more than one child for a particular letter, put them into alphabetical order using the second letters of their name.)
◆ *Which letter do we use for writing our name: capital or small?*
◆ *Why?* (Because you are important, so your name is important, and it has a big, important capital letter at the beginning.)
◆ *Whose name begins with this letter?* (Point to a letter on the poster and ask those children to stand up.)
◆ *Can you write the letter in the air?*
◆ *Who can cover a letter* (with a Post-it note) *that we didn't use?*

ASSESSMENT
Can the children identify the initial sounds at the beginning of their names? Are they also able to recognize the capital letters for their names?

WHAT SOUND DO WE MAKE FOR THIS LETTER?

GROUP SIZE AND ORGANIZATION
Whole class sitting in a semicircle facing the poster (YR/Y1; P1/2).
DURATION
Ten minutes.
LEARNING OBJECTIVES
To identify the sounds represented by particular letters. To be able to name something that begins with each letter sound.

YOU WILL NEED
The 'Alphabet train' poster, a set of lower case letter cards, photocopied from pages 8–10.

WHAT TO DO
Place the letter cards face down in a pile in the middle of the semicircle. Pick one of the children to take a card from the pile and say, for example: 'My card has a 't' for table on it. Who can point to the 't' on the train?' The child with the card chooses another child to point to the truck. If the second child points to the correct truck on the poster, he or she picks up the next card. The previous card goes back, on the bottom of the pile. Keep playing until everyone has had a go. The children may need reminding that they need to make sure that everyone has a turn.

ASSESSMENT
Check that each child is able to match his or her letter shape to an item. It is important to praise a child who makes a 'mistake' such as 'c' for 'queen'.

IDEAS FOR DIFFERENTIATION
If particular letters give difficulty, make a 'judicious' card selection of your own (of a tricky letter) and ask the children to think of things that begin with that letter. Target the less able children, challenging them individually to 'name something beginning with "d"' and so on.

EXTENSION WORK
The game can be extended to include the digraphs 'sh', 'ch' and 'th'.

Teach/remind the children of how to play 'I spy' and have one round each day.

WORDS

GROUP SIZE AND ORGANIZATION
Whole class sitting in a semicircle, facing a flip chart or a large sheet of paper and a shared text (YR/Y1; P1/2).
DURATION
About ten minutes as a whole-class demonstration, then ten minutes paired work.
LEARNING OBJECTIVE
To write words to correspond with initial letter sounds.

YOU WILL NEED
A flip chart or a large sheet of paper, marker pen, a shared reading text, reading books appropriate to the children's independent abilities, paper, pencils.

WHAT TO DO
Read a page from the shared text as a class. Ask the children to choose a word with more than five letters from the text. Write this word vertically on the flip chart. Ask the children to suggest words that begin with each of the letters written vertically. The children should be encouraged to use other words from the shared text if possible. You may want to write several words for each letter.

Ask the children to work in pairs with their own reading books and paper to carry out a similar activity. It is important that they are able to read their words and to spell them correctly. (Using their own texts should encourage this independence.)

The activity could be extended by asking the children to rewrite the words in alphabetical order.

ASSESSMENT
Check that the children are matching words to initial sounds.

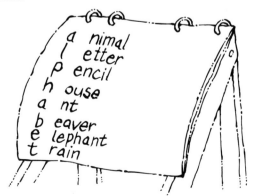

Middle sounds/vowels

VOWEL SEARCH

GROUP SIZE AND ORGANIZATION
Whole class sitting in a semicircle facing the poster (YR/Y1; P1/2).
DURATION
15 minutes.
LEARNING OBJECTIVE
To distinguish between vowels and consonants.

YOU WILL NEED
The 'Alphabet train' poster, a flip chart or a large sheet of paper pinned up nearby, marker pen.

WHAT TO DO
Ask the children to look at the wheels of the trucks on the poster carefully. Ask them:
◆ *What do you notice?* (Red and yellow wheels.)
◆ *Who can point to a truck with red wheels? And another?*
◆ *How many are there? Let's count them together.* (…Five!)
◆ *Can we say their letter names together?* (a, e, i, o, u.)

Explain that these letters are called 'vowels' and write them on the flip chart. The children will need to know that we may say their letter names or letter sounds when they are at the beginning of words. Write words beginning with vowel sounds and names: 'A' is for 'Andrew' (sound) and 'Amy' (name); 'E' is for 'Emma' and 'Edith'; 'I' is for 'Isabel' and 'Ivy'; 'O' is for 'Oliver' and 'Oberon'; 'U' is for 'Uncle Ulysses'.

You may want to look at the picture cards for initial vowels (on photocopiable page 21) to help establish that vowels use their sound and their name. Write the children's ideas on the flip chart and read them in unison, identifying whether the vowel is being used as its name or sound.

Then ask:
◆ *Who can see a truck that has wheels that are not all yellow or all red?*
◆ *What is the name of the letter?*
◆ *Who knows what letter we write at the end of 'mummy' or 'daddy'?*

Write the word 'mummy' on the sheet and identify the last letter as 'y'. Explain that in the word mummy, 'y' is pretending to be the vowel 'e' at the end of the word. You may like to tell the children that it plays a similar trick at the end of 'my', 'by', 'try' and 'cry' too, but here it steals another vowel's sound:

◆ *Which vowel sound is 'y' stealing in 'my'?* ('i'.)
Revise the vowel names and sounds together.

ASSESSMENT

Check that the children can recognize 'a', 'e', 'i', 'o' and 'u' as 'vowels' and know that these letters may be spoken as their letter names or sounds in words.

FINGER VOWELS

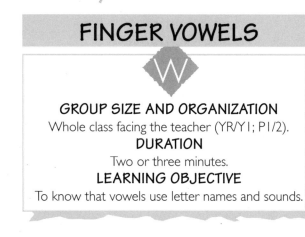

GROUP SIZE AND ORGANIZATION
Whole class facing the teacher (YR/Y1; P1/2).
DURATION
Two or three minutes.
LEARNING OBJECTIVE
To know that vowels use letter names and sounds.

YOU WILL NEED

The vowel letter cards photocopied from page 21 (pinned up) and/or the 'Alphabet train' poster.

WHAT TO DO

Hold out both your hands in front of you with your fists loosely clenched, lift the thumb of your left hand and say 'a for apron' (using the letter name). Touch this thumb with the thumb of your right hand and say 'a for apple' (using the letter sound). Raise the index finger of your left hand and say, 'e for emu' and match it up with the index finger from your right hand saying, 'e for egg.' Continue raising and matching the fingers of your left hand with the fingers of your right, using vowel names and sounds. The children will soon start to copy you and want to prompt you. This is excellent as a quick reminder of the vowels or to reinforce the significance of vowels.

ASSESSMENT

Check that the children are suggesting words that use the correct letter.

CAN YOU HEAR THE VOWEL?

GROUP SIZE AND ORGANIZATION
A group of about ten children (YR/Y1; P1/2).
DURATION
About ten minutes.
LEARNING OBJECTIVE
To be able to identify the middle letter (vowel) in CVC words.

YOU WILL NEED

A set of vowel cards for each child, photocopied from page 8. You may also want to use pictures that illustrate the words you use. (You could choose some examples from those on photocopiable page 21.)

WHAT TO DO

Hearing the beginning sound in words is the easiest for children and with practice most are able to hear the final phoneme. Listening for the middle letter is the most difficult, even in CVC words. (Do not use words with difficult phonemes at this stage.) The vowel sounds will need to be overemphasized and mouth shapes carefully observed.

Distribute the vowel cards. Ask the children to listen carefully and show you the vowel card that represents the sound they can hear in the middle of the words you say. Try these words, one at a time:

Tip, tap, top, tep, tup,
Bit, bat, bot, bet, but,
Bag, beg, big, bog, bug,
Bin, ben, ban, bon, bun.

It is important that children are able to identify the sounds in nonsense words as these often form syllables in more complex words (for example, 'tep', 'tepid', 'step').

ASSESSMENT

Are the children able to identify the vowel sound in the middle of a word?

JIGSAW SNAKE VOWELS AND CONSONANTS

W

GROUP SIZE AND ORGANIZATION
Whole class sitting in a semicircle (YR/Y1; P1/2).
DURATION
Five minutes.
LEARNING OBJECTIVE
To consolidate knowledge of vowels and consonants.

YOU WILL NEED
The 'Alphabet train' poster, Post-it notes, 'Jigsaw snake' poster and the children's own completed alphabet snake jigsaws (see 'Jigsaw letters' on page 4), flip chart or a large sheet of paper, felt-tipped pens, red and yellow crayons.

WHAT TO DO
Ask the class if they can remember why some of the trucks on the alphabet train have different coloured wheels:
◆ *Who can remember what the letters in the red-wheeled trucks are called?*
◆ *How many vowels are there?*
◆ *What sounds and names do they have?*
◆ *Who can come and cover the vowels with Post-it notes?*
◆ *Who can write the vowels on my sheet of paper?*
Turn over the A1 poster and ask who can point to the vowels on the jumbled snake. Let the children work in pairs for about ten minutes to colour the edges of the vowel segments of their snakes in red and the consonant segments in yellow.

ASSESSMENT
Can the children identify the vowels in the alphabet?

EXTENSION WORK
If they have time, the children could draw objects beginning with the vowel sounds and vowel names to be displayed with their coloured-in posters.

End sounds

WHO CAN HEAR THE END LETTER?

GROUP SIZE AND ORGANIZATION
A group of about ten children sitting in a semicircle (YR/Y1; P1/2).
DURATION
About ten minutes.
LEARNING OBJECTIVE
To be able to match end letter sounds to a letter on the 'Alphabet train' poster.

YOU WILL NEED
The 'Alphabet train' poster. (You may want to show pictures of CVC words used in this activity, such as 'tin', 'pot', 'bag'. Try not to use words that end with a double-letter sound, for example 'ar' in 'car'.)

WHAT TO DO
Ask the children to listen carefully as you say each word; they are listening especially for the last letter in the word. Say the word slowly, emphasizing each phoneme and say, for example, 'Who can point to the letter that has the sound you can hear at the end of the word "bed"?'

ASSESSMENT
Can the children hear the final phoneme and identify the letter shape that represents the sound made?

LETTER SOUNDS

WORD CHAINS

GROUP SIZE AND ORGANIZATION
Whole class sitting in a semicircle (YR/Y1; P1/2).
DURATION
About 15 minutes.
LEARNING OBJECTIVES
To be able to hear and identify beginning and end letters in a word. To use the end letter to begin a new word.

YOU WILL NEED
The 'Alphabet train' poster, a flip chart or a large sheet of paper, marker pen.

WHAT TO DO
Ask the first child in the semicircle to give you a word (for example, 'dog'). Before writing the word on the flip chart, ask:
◆ *What letter can you hear at the beginning of the word 'dog'?* ('d'.)
◆ *Can you find the letter on the 'Alphabet train' poster?*
◆ *Can anyone hear the last letter in the word 'dog'? What is the letter?* ('g'.)
◆ *Who can find 'g' on the alphabet train?*
Write the word and establish that the word ends with 'g'. Now ask the next child to give you a word starting with 'g'. Again, identify its initial and end letters. Continue writing this chain until everyone has had a turn: 'dog–got–top–plant–time–egg…' Highlight the last/first letters. You may like to write all the letters that you used in a separate list and tally their frequency.
◆ *Which letters did we use most/least?*
◆ *Why do you think some letters were not used?*
You may want to discuss that each word contains at least one vowel. (This activity will help the children with the next activity, 'Hangman'.)

ASSESSMENT
Are the children able to hear and identify the last letter in CVC words or those that have an easily identifiable final letter?

EXTENSION WORK
Ask the children:
◆ *Which vowels have we used most?*
◆ *Which end letters are the most/least popular?*

HANGMAN

GROUP SIZE AND ORGANIZATION
A group of up to ten children (YR/Y1; P1/2).
DURATION
Ten minutes.
LEARNING OBJECTIVE
To use their knowledge of letter frequency to identify words.

YOU WILL NEED
The 'Alphabet train' poster, a Big Book, a flip chart or a large sheet of paper pinned up nearby, marker pen, Post-it notes (optional).

WHAT TO DO
(The children's knowledge gained in the previous activity, 'Word chains', will help them with this activity.) Read a page from the Big Book with the children. Secretly choose a word from the text and draw short horizontal lines on the flip chart to represent each of the letters in the word. Ask:
◆ *How many letters does the word have?*
◆ *Which words on the page could it be?*
Read the possible words together. You may want to write them on a separate sheet of paper. Ask the children to look at the words carefully and put their hands up when they have thought of a letter that might be in your word. Is the letter in more than one word?
Enter the letter onto a line in the word or begin to draw the gallows. It is important that the children are encouraged to work systematically. You may want to begin eliminating words from the page of the Big Book by covering them with Post-it notes.

ASSESSMENT
Identify those that are guessing wildly. They will need extra opportunities for listening to letter sounds in words or playing word chains in a small group.

LETTER SOUNDS

Initial letter name and sound pictures

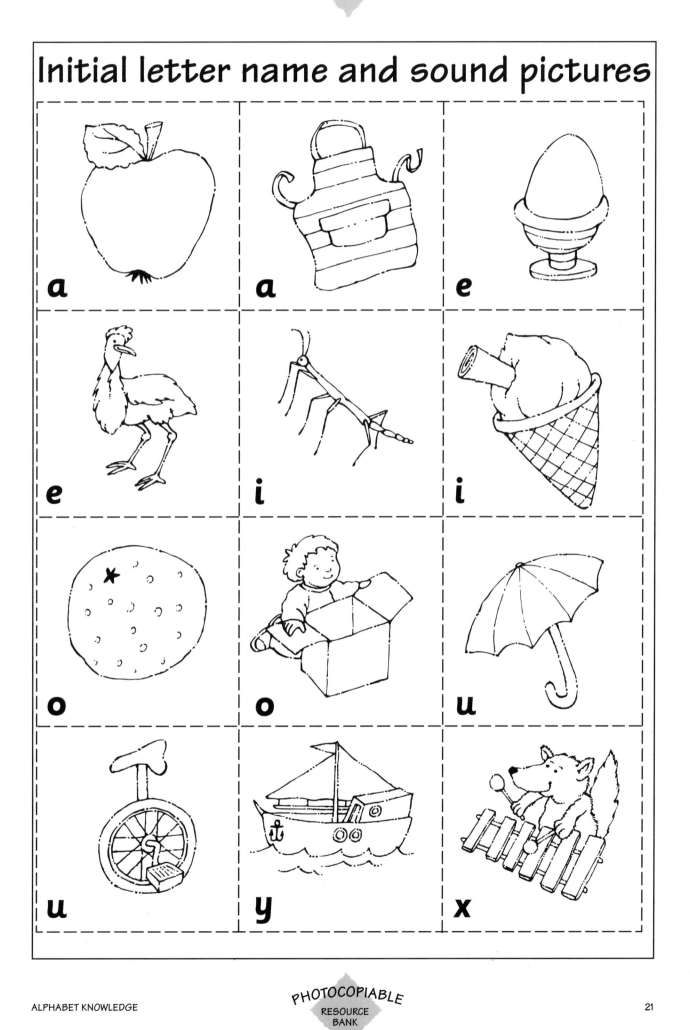

a

a

e

e

i

i

o

o

u

u

y

x

PHOTOCOPIABLE
RESOURCE
BANK

LETTER SOUNDS

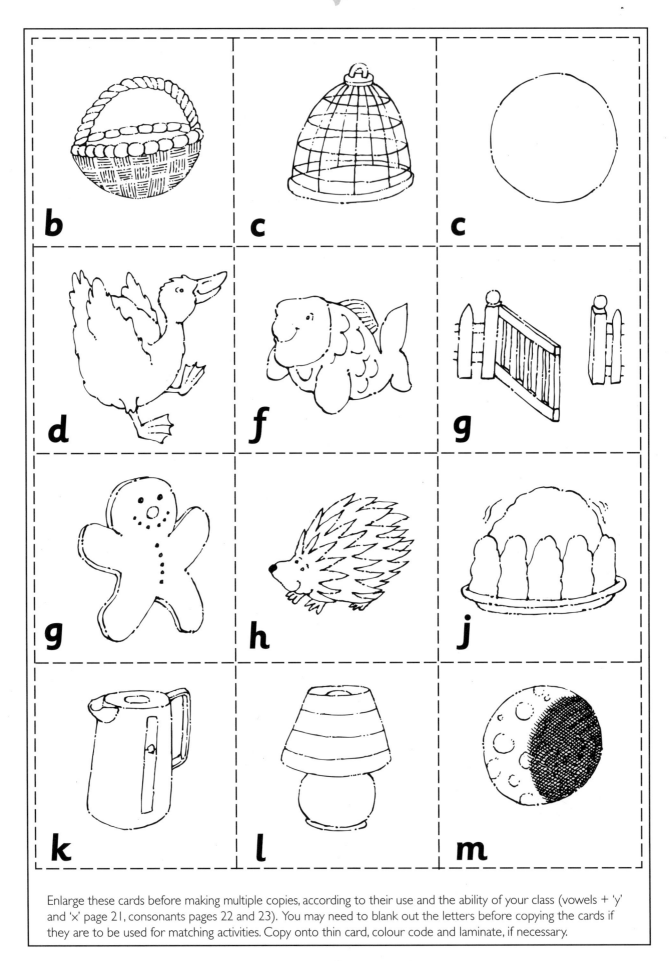

Enlarge these cards before making multiple copies, according to their use and the ability of your class (vowels + 'y' and 'x' page 21, consonants pages 22 and 23). You may need to blank out the letters before copying the cards if they are to be used for matching activities. Copy onto thin card, colour code and laminate, if necessary.

PHOTOCOPIABLE
RESOURCE
BANK

LETTER SOUNDS

n

p

q

r

s

t

v

w

z

sh

ch

th

The alphabet picture cards on pages 21–23 are: apple, apron, egg, emu, insect, ice-cream, orange, open, umbrella, unicycle, yacht, fox playing a xylophone; basket, cage, circle, duck, fish, gate, gingerbread man, hedgehog, jelly, kettle, lamp, moon; nine, plate, queen, rabbit, star; tree, violin, watch, zebra, shoe, cheese, thistle.

WRITING SKILLS

SAND TRAY LETTERS

GROUP SIZE AND ORGANIZATION
A group of about six children (YR/Y1; P1/2).
DURATION
Up to ten minutes.
LEARNING OBJECTIVES
To identify the spoken letter and then to be able to write the correct lower case letter.

YOU WILL NEED
A shallow tray of washed sand for each child.

WHAT TO DO
Ask the children to draw the beginning letter of a word, for example 'book', in the sand.
◆ *What letter have you written?*
◆ *How did you write the letter?* (Top to bottom, halfway back up and round.)
Ask the children to smooth the sand and try other letters. You may want to practise letters with a similar writing shape (or family).

ASSESSMENT
Make sure that the children are forming their letters correctly.

PAINTING THE 'C' LETTER FAMILY

GROUP SIZE AND ORGANIZATION
A group of about ten children (YR/Y1; P1/2).
DURATION
30 minutes.
LEARNING OBJECTIVE
To form correctly the letters in the 'c' writing family: 'c', 'a', 'd', 'g' and 'q'. (You may want to add 'o' to this letter-writing family.)

YOU WILL NEED
Finger-paints and paper for each child, a flip chart or a large sheet of paper, marker pen.

WHAT TO DO
Demonstrate writing the 'c' shape on the flip chart. It often helps if you show what happens if you don't begin the shape well over to the right. Ask the children

to draw in the air with you before trying to write the letter with the finger-paints.
Repeat with 'a'. Encourage the children to say: 'Start like a "c", then go all the way round to join up, then straight down.' Remind the children that this letter is one continuous movement. Practise it several times until the shape is almost perfect.
Continue until all the letters have been painted. The children may like to paint pictures to represent their letters.

ASSESSMENT
Look at the children's writing to check that the letters in the 'c' writing family are formed correctly. If the children are finding them difficult, practise one letter at a time. It may help to practise with a copy of photocopiable page 28.

PLASTICINE SNAKES

GROUP SIZE AND ORGANIZATION
A group of ten children (YR/Y1; P1/2).
DURATION
Ten minutes.
LEARNING OBJECTIVES
To become familiar with the 's' shape.

YOU WILL NEED
Enough Plasticine (or dough) for each child to make a 'sausage' about 20cm long, an 's' shape printed on A5 card for each child.

WHAT TO DO
The 's' shape is difficult to write; it begins on the right, the same as the 'c' shape (unlike the numbers '2' and '3'), and has a double bend that is similar to writing '2'. Ask the children what letter shape they can see on the

card ('s'). Then tell them to use their index finger to draw the 's' shape in the air. Remind the children to begin at the top of the letter. Encourage 'ssss' sounds. Now ask the children to trace over the letter on their card. Let them roll out their Plasticine into a long thin 'sausage' shape and tell them to twist this shape over the 's' on the card.

They may like to draw 'six swimming swans' or use the handwriting sheet on photocopiable page 28 to practise the letter 's'.

ASSESSMENT
Check for correct formation and letter sound to correspond with 's'.

PAINTING THE SILLY 'e'

GROUP SIZE AND ORGANIZATION
A group of ten children (YR/Y1; P1/2).
DURATION
20 minutes.
LEARNING OBJECTIVE
To write the less conventional letter shape of 'e'.

YOU WILL NEED
Finger-paints (or broad felt-tipped pens), a copy of a large 'e' shape (where the starting point is clearly marked with an arrow indicating the direction) for each child.

WHAT TO DO
Writing the letter 'e' is very difficult for small children. It requires special attention. The children need to be told where to begin their 'e' shape. Ask the children to write the letter in the air, following your hand movement, before using paint or pens.

ASSESSMENT
Are the children writing the 'e' shape in one movement?

EXTENSION WORK
Use the photocopiable handwriting sheet on page 29 to help children practise this shape.

MAKING A 'k'

GROUP SIZE AND ORGANIZATION
A group of ten children (YR/Y1; P1/2).
DURATION
10 minutes.
LEARNING OBJECTIVE
To know that two parts are needed to form the letter 'k'.

YOU WILL NEED
Enough Plasticine (or dough) for each child to make a 'sausage' 15–20cm long, an A5 card printed with the letter 'k' for each child.

WHAT TO DO
This is another letter that causes problems. The straight-down movement is easy, however knowing where to start for the 'arrow' part is difficult.
Ask the children:
◆ *Which letter is written on your card?* ('k'.)
◆ *Which words begin with this letter?*
◆ *Which other letter in the alphabet makes the same sound in words?* ('c'.)
◆ *How many pieces of Plasticine do you think you will need to make the 'k'?* (Two, although it may look like three.)

Let the children make their letters on the cards. Then ask them to trace over the letters with their fingers, making two lines.

ASSESSMENT
Check that the children are able to form the letter 'k' correctly with two lines (l and <) and are aware that it represents the same letter sound as 'c'.

WRITING SKILLS

FEELY FOOTSTEPS

GROUP SIZE AND ORGANIZATION
Individuals working independently (YR/Y1; P1/2).
DURATION
About 20 minutes.
LEARNING OBJECTIVE
To become familiar with the letter shapes.

Can you work out which letter I am?

YOU WILL NEED
Art paper, pencils, letter templates, glue, scissors, washed sand (or lentils, rice and so on).

WHAT TO DO
Make feet shapes by asking each child to draw around his or her shoe and cut out the shape; find a letter template (lower case) and draw around it inside the foot shape; cover the letter shape with glue; sprinkle sand onto the letter, shake off the excess and allow to dry.

When dry, these letters can be used for a variety of purposes:
◆ Arrange them as an alphabet.
◆ Let the children practise writing letter shapes by feeling over the letter shapes.
◆ Draw an imaginary letter on the wall while the children watch, then the child who has that 'foot' letter must say: 'I'm the "e" for egg,' and then trace round the shape.

ASSESSMENT
Can the children write the letter shapes correctly in response to the letter names or sounds?

WHICH IS TODAY'S LETTER?

GROUP SIZE AND ORGANIZATION
A group of about ten children sitting on the carpet in two rows (YR/Y1; P1/2).
DURATION
Five minutes.
LEARNING OBJECTIVE
To identify a letter by its shape.

YOU WILL NEED
A flip chart or a large sheet of paper, marker pen.

WHAT TO DO
Choose one child and trace a letter on his or her back with your finger (for example, 't'). If the child is able to say it is 't for table', for example, ask the child to write the letter on the flip chart. Watch for correct letter formation.

Ask all the children to write the letter in the air with you. It often helps to say: 'Start at the top, straight down with a little hook, pick up your pencil and cross the 't'. Then ask:
◆ *Who can tell me something else beginning with 't'?*
Repeat with other children and new letters. The children could go on to work in pairs, taking turns to write pretend letters on each other's backs to guess.

ASSESSMENT
Check that the children are able to identify letters by their shape and match them to the correct sounds.

EXTENSION WORK
Use copies of photocopiable pages 27–29 to help children form the letters correctly.

Name _____   Date _____

The top to bottom writing family

◆ Trace over and continue writing these letters in several different colours.
Always start at the dot.

i i i i
straight down and dot the 'i'

t t t t
straight down, and cross the 't'

l l l l
straight down

n n n n
down, up and over

m m m m
down, up and over, up and over

r r r r
down, up and over a bit

h h h h
down, halfway up and over

b b b b
down, halfway up, round and close it

u u u u u
down, under, up and down

y y y y
down, under, up and down with a hook

j j j j
down with a hook and dot the top

PHOTOCOPIABLE
RESOURCE
BANK

Name _____ Date _____

The 'c' writing family

◆ Trace over and continue writing these letters in several different colours.
Always start at the dot.

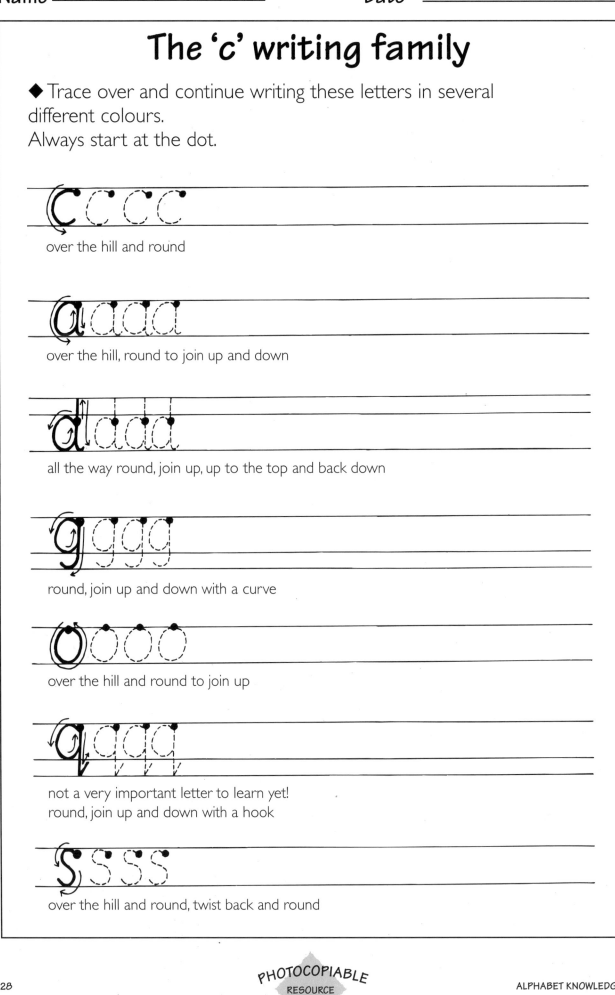

over the hill and round

over the hill, round to join up and down

all the way round, join up, up to the top and back down

round, join up and down with a curve

over the hill and round to join up

not a very important letter to learn yet!
round, join up and down with a hook

over the hill and round, twist back and round

ALPHABET KNOWLEDGE

Name ——————————————— Date ———————————

Hard letters

◆ Trace over and continue writing these letters in several different colours.
Always start at the dot.

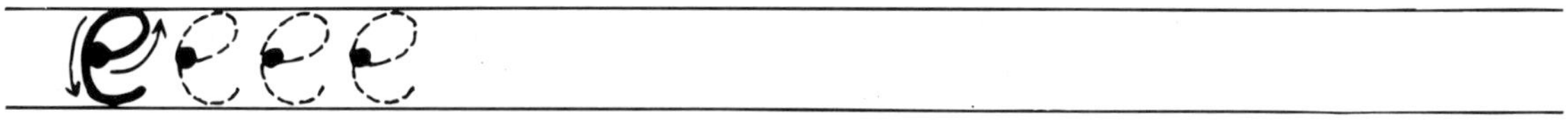

e e e e

start at the middle, curve up and round, almost like a 'c' shape

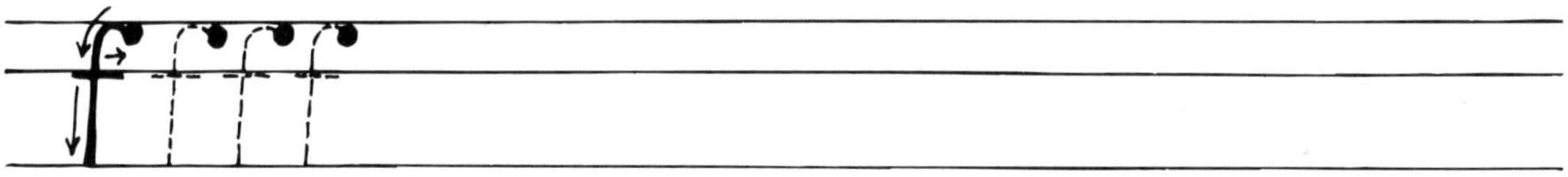

f f f f

hook at the top, down, pencil off and cross

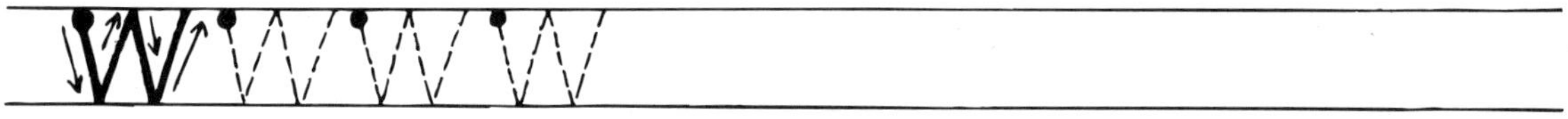

w w w w

down, up and down, up

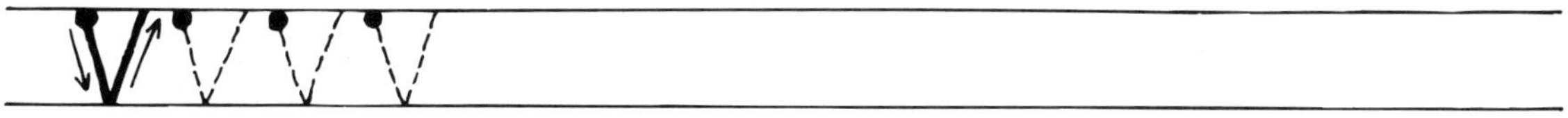

v v v v

down and up

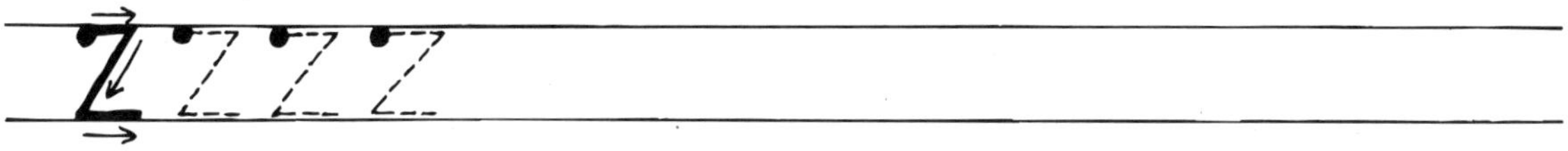

z z z z

across, down and across

k k k k

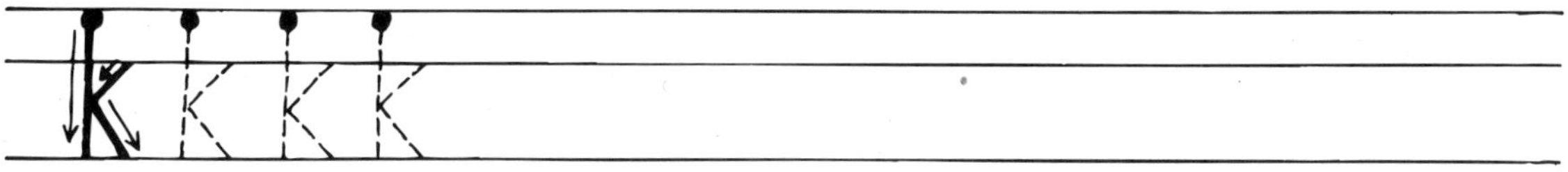

straight down, now make a sideways 'v'

DICTIONARY SKILLS

WORD SEARCH

GROUP SIZE AND ORGANIZATION
Explain the task with the whole class sitting in a semicircle facing the 'Alphabet train' poster. Then move into pairs (Y1/2; P2/3).
DURATION
About ten minutes for the whole-class introduction; 15 minutes for the paired work.
LEARNING OBJECTIVE
To enable the children to arrange words in alphabetical order.

YOU WILL NEED
For the whole-class introduction: the 'Alphabet train' poster, a Big Book, felt-tipped pens, large Post-it notes; for the paired work: spare paper, pencils, a suitable reading book for each pair of children.

WHAT TO DO
Introduce the lesson by reading a page from the shared text. Ask a child to point to a word from the text. Read the word together and write it on a Post-it note (for example, 'donkey'). Ask for another word from the text beginning with a different letter. Repeat this until you have about eight words, written on Post-it notes, all beginning with different letters. You may need to include only words beginning with simple letter sounds. Read them in unison, then ask the children to help you arrange the words in alphabetical order:

◆ *Which word will we need to put first?* ('donkey', for example.) *Why?*

Check the answer on the poster by reading the letters up to 'd' (for 'donkey').

◆ *Which word should we put next?* ('friend', for example.) *How do you know?*

Again, check by reading along the alphabet train, emphasizing 'd' as it is passed and reinforcing that there is no 'e' word on the Post-it notes that should go next instead.

Repeat until all the Post-it notes are in the correct order. Finally, check the finished sequence by reading the alphabet letters and the vocabulary.

Now the children should work in pairs to find and copy their own six words from their reading books and to arrange the resulting Post-it notes in alphabetical order. Whether you leave the poster on view as an aid will depend on the children's confidence.

Encourage the children to move to sit in fours and re-order their 12 words.

At the end of the session (in the plenary, if appropriate), ask the children to work, in groups of eight, to arrange their 24 words for the class to share. Check as a class using the 'Alphabet train' poster.

ASSESSMENT
Can all the children arrange words into alphabetical order by initial letter?

IDEAS FOR DIFFERENTIATION
Ask more able children to find six words beginning with the same initial letter and order them. You will need to explain to the children how to tackle this task.

Less able children should start with two or three words and then fit others into the order, one at a time.

GETTING INTO ALPHABETICAL ORDER

GROUP SIZE AND ORGANIZATION
Whole class (Y1/2; P2/3).
DURATION
15 minutes.
LEARNING OBJECTIVE
To be able to extend using alphabetical order to arrange words that all begin with the same letter.

YOU WILL NEED
The 'Alphabet train' poster, flip chart or large sheet of paper, large Post-it notes, marker pen.

WHAT TO DO
Ask the children to choose a letter from the 'Alphabet train' poster (try to avoid vowels and 'x' and 'z'). Then ask for some words beginning with the letter chosen, for example 's'. Write the words, in large letters, on individual Post-it notes and display them on the flip chart where all the children can see them.

Ask the children how you can arrange these words into alphabetical order:
◆ *Will the first letter help us?*
◆ *Why/why not?*

Ask the children to suggest how they can be ordered. Refer to the 'Alphabet train' poster as you direct them to the second letters. You may find that

RESOURCE BANK

you will need to look at the third letters. Conclude by asking the children to take a Post-it note, each one with a different letter on it, and line up in order. Use the 'Alphabet train' poster for checking.

ASSESSMENT
Make sure the children understand how the second letter of a word is used to sort out alphabetical order if initial letters are the same.

WHAT IS A DICTIONARY?

GROUP SIZE AND ORGANIZATION
A group of about eight children (Y1/2; P2/3).
DURATION
15 minutes.
LEARNING OBJECTIVE
To understand the organization and use of a dictionary.

YOU WILL NEED
A dictionary for every child, the 'Alphabet train' poster, a Big Book or other shared text (optional).

WHAT TO DO
It is useful, but not essential, to start this activity with a shared reading text. 'Stumble' over a word and consider what it might mean. Ask the children how they might find out, guiding them towards looking it up in a dictionary.

Ask the children if they know what a dictionary is for and how we use it. Go on to discuss an example:
◆ *If you were looking for a word beginning with 'a' where do you think you might begin to look? Why?*
◆ *What about 's'?*
◆ *Is it near the beginning, middle or end of the alphabet?*
You may want to suggest that they look at the 'Alphabet train' poster for clues.

Then ask them:
◆ *Why do we need to know where a letter is in the alphabet?* (To know where to start looking for a word.)
◆ *Who can find the word 'cat' in the dictionary?* (Remind the children to think about roughly where they should open the dictionary to begin with.)
◆ *Who can read the explanation of the word?*
Give strategies:
◆ *Will it be near the middle, near the beginning or near the end? If you are looking for a word beginning with 'h' and you open the dictionary at 'j', will you need to go forwards or back?*

Alternatively, focus on the spelling support of a dictionary and query the spelling of a word during shared writing. Work through the same questioning process, but to check your 'questionable' spelling, rather than to identify meaning.

ASSESSMENT
Check that all the children have some idea of where to open the dictionary before attempting to look for a word.

IDEAS FOR DIFFERENTIATION
If the children are struggling with finding their way, go back and revise some of the earlier alphabetical order activities (see pages 4, 5, 7, 14, 15 and 16).

LOOKING UP WORDS

GROUP SIZE AND ORGANIZATION
A group of about eight children (Y2; P3).
DURATION
20 minutes.
LEARNING OBJECTIVE
To use a dictionary to find the meanings of words.

YOU WILL NEED
A dictionary for every child, the 'Alphabet train' poster and a list (of about four) words for each pair of children (preferably identified from their shared or group reading), scrap paper (optional), pencils, paper or English/spelling books.

WHAT TO DO
Ask the children to put the words in the list into alphabetical order and to find them in the dictionary. They could write the words onto individual pieces of paper to physically move them about to help with the ordering. They should copy each word and its definition into their books.

ASSESSMENT
Were the children able to find the words and copy the definitions?

DICTIONARY SKILLS

WHAT IS AN INDEX?

GROUP SIZE AND ORGANIZATION
A group of about eight children (Y2; P3).
DURATION
20 minutes.
LEARNING OBJECTIVE
To find out about indexes.

YOU WILL NEED
A non-fiction book for sharing (any book that has a contents page and an index, such as a poetry or song book; a Big Book containing these features would be useful).

WHAT TO DO
Look at the book together and ask the children, for example:
◆ *Can anyone find the rhyme 'Humpty Dumpty' for me in this book?*
◆ *Where would be the best place to look first?*
◆ *Is there anything in the book that might help me to find the rhyme quickly?*

Look through the book, refer to the contents page at the front and compare it with the index at the back. Generally, the contents only list the main sections (chapters) in page order, whereas the index lists topics within each section or chapter arranged alphabetically. An index may be arranged in two, or sometimes three, ways within the same book. In a poetry book, for example, the first lines of the poems are usually arranged in alphabetical order; the titles of the poems may appear in a separate index; and thirdly, the poems may be categorized into different subjects, listed in alphabetical order.

Ask the children:
◆ *Which is the most useful when you want to find a particular rhyme, the index or the contents list?*
◆ *Can you explain how the contents page and index pages are the same?*
◆ *How are they different?*
◆ *Why are both needed in a book?*
◆ *What type of books need an index? Why?*

You may want the children to have access to a wide range of non-fiction books to compare the indexes in them and how they are arranged.

ASSESSMENT
Are the children able to explain how an index works and why it is necessary? Are they clear about the differences between an index and a contents list?

CAN YOU WRITE AN INDEX?

GROUP SIZE AND ORGANIZATION
A group of about eight children (Y2; P3).
DURATION
20 minutes.
LEARNING OBJECTIVE
To write an index for their own non-fiction booklets.

YOU WILL NEED
The children's own non-narrative booklets that they have written in a previous lesson; a factfile (or booklet) on themselves (or on a plant, animal or machine); a non-fiction book with an index; scrap paper; pencils.

WHAT TO DO
Hold up the non-fiction book and ask:
◆ *Can anyone tell me where I can find the index?*
◆ *What will I find in the index?*
◆ *How will it be arranged?*

Show the children the index and read through it with them.
◆ *How does the index work?*
◆ *What does the book need in order for me to use the index?* (Page numbers.)
◆ *What would be helpful in your factfile in order to write an index?* (Page numbers and headings.)

Ask the children to write an index for their own booklets. Before beginning they will need to write page numbers and headings. You may want them to use scrap paper for their first attempt.

ASSESSMENT
How successful were the children at writing suitable headings, page numbers and indexes for their booklets?

RESOURCE BANK

ALPHABET KNOWLEDGE